COMPUTER RECOVERY PLAN

Dougglas Hurtado Carmona

COMPUTER RECOVERY PLAN

Dougglas Hurtado Carmona
Doctor en gestión de la Innovación. Magister en Ingeniería de Sistemas y Computación, Ingeniero de Sistemas, Universidad del Norte. Docente Investigador y escritor. Fue Decano Facultad de Ingeniería de Sistemas.

Computer recovery plan

Translated from the first edition in Spanish

Dougglas Hurtado Carmona

2020, Copyright
ISBN (Print):   978-1-716-41489-3
ISBN (Digital): 978-1-716-36983-4

Contact: dougglas@gmail.com
              dougglas.hurtado@unad.edu.co

CONTENT

Introduction to the recovery plan

Objectives of the recovery plan

The general objective of the plan is to have a document with a series of instructions that allows to respond effectively to any interruption of the Data Processing Department, minimizing and impacting the activities of the entire organization. This basic objective is due to the current dependence of the service and the data maintained by these departments.

At the same time, the plan seeks to improve the safety conditions of employees and their resources, in order to safeguard both human assets and vital information (vital records), of the entire organization, of which the data center is only the custodian.

Additionally, the recovery plan ensures continuity of business operations. Based on tests previously carried out in an alternative center and of which there is documentation, which contains all the appropriate procedures for the restoration of the services previously established in the plan. The design and implementation of these procedures must respond effectively and reasonably to business interruptions involving the Data Center and its services.

A business interruption refers to the occurrence of an event that causes a severe impact on business processes, and that prevents the performance of a large part of its activities, impairing the processing of information, production or provision of services.

The recovery plan of an entity establishes the phases to be followed in the contingency plan development project. Basically the recovery plan has the following components:

- Education.
- Executives
- Interdisciplinary groups.
- All the employees
- Development.
- Recovery tests
- Documentation. (Contingency plan)
- Maintenance.

Description of the contingency plan

The contingency plan corresponds to the information necessary to initiate the recovery, or maintain continuity, of a company's operations after the declaration of a disaster. The plan in form must contain the following chapters.

Emergency program for major interruptions. It is the scheme in which the sequence of actions to be followed is established from the identification of the emergency to the restoration of the Computer Center facilities, in the original site or alternate location.

Recovery teams. Description of the work teams with their responsibilities before, during and after the emergency or contingency.

Data center requirements. Establishes the physical needs of the Computer Center to return to an adequate mode of operation. It includes the requirements of the room, electrical energy, air conditioning, equipment (CPU, I / O´ etc.), teleprocessing etc.

List of suppliers. Establishes who must meet the needs of the Data Center. Includes suppliers of new or used equipment, software, communications, office support equipment, stationery, etc.

Priority of processes or applications. Critical process or application recovery procedures that have been categorized in terms of relative importance. (Ranking). These procedures contain all the information that enables them to be put into service.

Protection of the media. Security mechanisms to protect and retain vital files, databases and in general the backup procedures (Back-up) of the entire company. The location of vital files is listed here.

Computer operation. Includes on / off procedures, programming, etc., that will operate under emergency conditions.

OS. It includes the needs for operational software and application software, as well as the necessary instructions for putting them into operation.

Access control and physical security. Categories of authority or authorizations to enter certain critical areas of the company that are identified in the emergency.

Software security. It establishes the restrictions on the use of the system and the administration of keys or passwords in emergency conditions.

Insurance plan. It establishes the insurance coverage, of protected assets.

Follow-up to the plan. Audit responsibilities to the plan, to make sure it is kept up to date. It is worth clarifying that updating the documentation may fall to a coordinator, but the responsibility for monitoring or auditing is the responsibility of each owner.

Plan maintenance. Establish a schedule of periodic updates, for example quarterly, semi-annually, etc.

Your department's recovery plan

A methodology that can facilitate the elaboration of the general contingency plan is to carry it out in each function or department. A prototype department can even be designated and use the development and experience of this group for implementation in the other areas.

If this form is accepted, the employees of that function or department should use the same phases of the general recovery plan, but focused on the vital processes or applications of their department. Some key questions to start working with are:

- How long can the department survive without data processing services?
- What are the vital processes or applications of the

department?

- What are the priorities of these processes or applications?

- What alternative mechanisms can I use to provide services to users or clients of this department?

- In how long can I reconstruct the basic information, which allows the recovery of the operation of this department?

- What resources, inputs or supplies do I have for the recovery of the operation?

- Where can I start rebuilding the apartment?

- What minimum facilities do I require for the reconstruction of the department and / or recovery of the operation?

These and many other questions will arise when the department's contingency plan is being developed.

In any case, in conjunction with the data processing department, they need to produce a disaster recovery plan. This requires close cooperation between the two departments.

Users of personal computers should remember that they, by working with some independence, are likely not considered in the department plan and should take into account that they may lose their information, if they do not transfer their important data to the central system, or if they do not back up your data to be saved in a different place than the usual one. Be sure to consult your manager to include your requirements.

Components of the organization

The hierarchical distribution of the organization allows a general knowledge of the entire company and the identification of its key officials, which is why it is essential to have an updated organization chart available. Within the organization, four basic components are defined that interact permanently:

Business processes. Set of functions that are performed in the area of a company, directed to achieve the objectives of the organization. (Provider - Pleased Value- customer)

Information. It is the food of business processes. Currently it should be considered as a basic and necessary asset for the operation of most of the processes.

Systems and equipment. The logical association of machines (HW) facilities (SW), to support business processes.

Human Resources. It is the most important resource or asset of the components of the organization. It is definitely the driver of the business process.

Just as we know the organization chart of the company, we must start the organization of an organization chart in disaster mode, since it is very possible that the activities of certain officials will be drastically modified. This organization chart is part of the documentation included in the contingency plan.

Information within security systems

Within current security schemes, the role that this department plays in information security is becoming very important. That is why it is necessary to redefine current policies to include procedures that allow an effective protection of company information.

In the current environment, with advanced technological development, the risks in the management of information increase, (information leaks, lack of protection of assets, loss of confidentiality, etc.) making it necessary that the facilities that the Data Center has are controlled through general security policies where assets or resources are identified, their value is judged, control and their form of protection are established.

The final objective of these policies is to make employees aware of the need to comply with the procedures or standards established to guarantee the protection of information, avoiding its misuse, unauthorized modifications, piracy, fraud or destruction. Regarding the recovery plan, its applicability is:

- **Policies.** It is an organizational obligation and inherent to managerial activity.

- **Rule.** A recovery program for basic (vital) processes should be established.

- **Guides**. Identification of the processes. Prioritization. Determine vital information. Update vital records. Assign resources. Take a resilience test

Barriers to the recovery plan

Developing a recovery plan implies additional, but very important, work at all levels of the organization, so to the extent that it affects the performers of certain tasks, this will have objections or objections that we will call the barriers to the plan, let's see which ones. They can be from the different areas of the company:

- **Senior Management**. Confusion in the concept. The belief that Data processing is the Processor. Interference with other activities.

- **Middle management**. It is not in the annual plan. Add controls. It does not generate income.

- **Users**. Lack of awareness. Resistance to changes. Increase the workload

Additionally, there are other general barriers to all areas: on the one hand, the need for new resources such as user education, training, maintenance, the possible increase in staff and that the cost / benefit ratio is not tangible at first glance. . On the other hand, there is a generalized excess of confidence, since it is usually thought that it can never happen to us, or why precisely to us?

All these barriers must be overcome through the general development of the plan in such a way that the group that will lead the implementation, is the vehicle for promotion or dissemination, to make all other employees aware of the need to know the Recovery Plan.

Vital processes and applications

Identification of vital processes

Purpose

Identify through the representatives of the operating units (departments, sections, etc.) what the general business processes are, based on corporate objectives. From this annex, a selection should be initiated that allows establishing which are the vital processes that should be recovered in the event of a contingency. The evaluation questionnaire in this section will be very useful in the selection criteria.

Application

The identification of both the general processes and the vital processes of the function of the entire organization, of the executives (either directly or by delegation in the operating units), heads of division, department or section, etc.

Evaluation of the impact of the loss of vital processes

Purpose

The primary purpose is to help a process owner make business judgments. These business judgments have to do with the impact to the organization of the loss of a process.

Application

It is incumbent on all processes that require classification in the vital category. The following questionnaire should be used as a means of discussion between the owner and the person responsible for the recovery plan for this process. It can also help the director to validate which are the most critical business functions and in which applications they are supported.

Vital Process Assessment Questionnaire

Name of process:	
Owner:	
Question	**Choices**
Organizational impact: The loss of this process has the following impact on the company:	a. Catastrophic in the company or in some departments. b. Catastrophic from one to three departments. c. Moderate in the company. d. Moderate in the company. e. Minor in the company or in some departments.
With the loss of this process, how long can your department continue to perform all its functions without the usual data processing support? Assume that the loss of data processing support occurred during your peak workload.	a. Up to three days. b. Up to a week. c. Up to a month. d. More? Please specify:

Choose only one.	
Please indicate your highest workload periods during a specific month or during the week, if there are any for this process.	Months JFMAMJJASOND Days MTWTFSS Other peak workload considerations:
You have developed / established alternate procedures, manual or otherwise, that can be used to continue operations in case the normal process cannot be carried out normally.	......IF NOT If the answer is YES, the procedures have been tested ... a. During the last six months b. During the past year c. During the year before last d. Have not been tested
Use the following values for the economic impact assessment in the next three questions. (The values are modifiable according to a criterion that is previously established).	a. 1. More than $ 1,000,000,000 b. 2. Between $ 100,000,000 - $ 1,000,000,000 c. 3. Between $ 10,000,000 - $ 100,000,000 d. Four. Between $ 1,000,000 - $ 10,000,000 e. 5. Up to $ 1,000,000
Loss of this process may result in loss of income or additional expenses for royalties, interest, penalties, surcharges etc.	a. From the first day b. From the third day c. From the first week. d. From the second week e. From the first month
Losing this process can erode our customer base over a	a. From the first day b. From the third day

period of time. The cost to the organization of the lost business begins:	c. From the first week. d. From the second week e. From the first month
Losing this process can lead to fines and surcharges due to government requirements (state, local etc.) and starts:	a. From the first day b. From the third day c. From the first week. d. From the second week e. From the first month
The loss of this process may have legal consequences due to	tax regulations, contractual commitments, etc. Specify in morals of the personnel under your responsibility
The loss of this process can have the following negative impact on the morale of the personnel under your responsibility:	
Specify any other factors that should be considered in assessing the impact of the loss of this process.	

Recovery plan considerations

Recovery plan officials

So far, the vital business processes have been identified but we have not defined those responsible for coordinating the plan or their functions. It is essential to clarify that these officials have a mission within the development of the plan and do not necessarily belong to the working groups that are defined below.

Director. He is the chief executive of the plan. It may be one or more senior executive level people who should be shown the progress of the plan. Their functions are:

- Give the necessary approvals to ensure the start of the recovery plan

- Make sure that the plan is developed in a previously established time. You can set time goals for different stages.

- Approve the completion of recovery tests. Recovery test is an exercise where the event of a contingency is simulated, where all alternative resources are used for the recovery of vital processes, even working in an alternative center or facility according to the coverage that you want to give it. This test can be pre-scheduled, or cited without informing the process owners and can include one or multiple processes.

- Periodically review that the plan is updated. From the result of the previously written test, the director will have a report that will show him how up-to-date the scheduled plan is and if the corrective actions requested from the previous tests were executed.

- Serve as the only authorized spokesperson, himself or by delegation, for statements to external media. (radio, press etc.)

Vital Process Owners. He is responsible to the director that there is a recovery plan for each vital process. Depending on the complexity of the process, it is possible that for its operation several applications are required that will also have their owner defined. The functions of the owner of vital processes are:

- Commit the users of the process (local and external) to keep up to date with the recovery plan.

- Ensure that there is a recovery plan for each vital business process.

- Ensure that the recovery plan for each process can:

- Identify information that is vital to retrieve including procedures, flow charts, and process flow. For data processing applications (centralized, distributed process, and end-user computing) include application programs, files, systems, operations, and procedures.

- Identify the requirements and service providers. - equipment, supplies, forms, source documents, space, support, transportation etc.

- Specify times.- What does it require during the first two days, two weeks, one month, etc.

- Document the service levels committing to the support services necessary to recover the process.

- Identify test criteria, and participants, analyze test risks, and take actions to reduce them.

- Regularly advise the other application owners in the preparation of the tests. For this you must:

- Revalidate or update the plan with the latest modifications that are delivered or with those that he himself has foreseen.

- Ensure that supporting information, located outside the

facilities, is kept up to date.

- Review the test results, anticipate new risks and, if necessary, indicate the corrective actions to take.
- Periodically prepare the recovery preparation report.
- This is a document that indicates how prepared you are for the event of a contingency.

Records and information manager. Its functions are:

- Ensure education about the business vital records program is conducted.
- Ensure that the owners who have developed the recovery plan for the vital departmental or functional business processes include all the required components and are protected off-site.
- Certify that vital business process owners have periodically reviewed the plans to update them and have submitted their recovery readiness reports for consolidated review by the local CEO.
- Confirm that the administrative and security controls during off-site storage and movement of the recovery plan, information and applications are adequate. Ensure that there is a procedure to identify risks and report them to owners.

General service providers. They are internal organizations that provide support services such as office services, physical space, transportation, communication, supplies, security, etc. Its functions are:

- Negotiate service level agreements with the owners of vital business processes, defining the services committed in the period following the disaster until normal operation is restored.

- Owners are responsible for identifying the maximum acceptable time for each step of the recovery.

- Prepare recovery plans covering service commitments and off-site protection.

Data processing service providers. In addition to the above requirements for all general service providers, data processing service providers must:

- Negotiate with the owners of vital business processes.

- The design of tests to demonstrate the recoverability with alternate facilities, using the information for protected off-site recovery.

- The frequency and programs of tests, where it should be done and the participants who will attend.

- Negotiate service level agreement in writing, with the managers of the alternate internal computing facilities, covering: The minimum level of service committed to each vital business process; Detailed configuration of processors, direct access storage devices, programs, telecommunication facilities, and other pertinent resources.

- Support staff, both in number and level of training required, in alternate facilities to meet the levels of service compromised both after a disaster and during

16

testing times.

- Notification procedures for changes in the data processing or support configuration, which may affect the recovery or agreed tests.

Vital process requirements

In conclusion, each vital process must meet the following requirements:

1. Qthat has an owner. Who has exactly identified the needs to recover their process and who has periodically updated, reviewed and verified their plan.

2. Whate has been tested. Each computer application with which a vital process is supported must be tested, therefore the owner and the data processing service provider must participate in the tests, to which the frequency and the site have been set in advance. More about vital applications will be discussed in the next section.

3. That it is documented. All those revisions, verifications or updates must be documented in the recovery readiness report.

Four. That the operating needs are considered. Supplies, communications, data processing equipment, support equipment., Space.

5. That the c are definedinterdepartmental commitments. (IT, Shopping, Services, Engineering, Physical security or industrial security)

17

So far, we have identified the vital processes, they have been evaluated according to a questionnaire, the plan officials have been defined and especially the owners of each vital process and the requirements of each of these processes have been reviewed.

The vital applications

As seen previously, each process is supported in one or more applications and now we are going to make the selection of the vital applications according to certain information conditions.

Information as a means of selection

Information is a group of data logically associated to carry out or manage a process. Every process works with three basic types of information:

- Generated and used by the same process.
- Generated by other processes.
- Generated by being used in other processes

The information can reside in:

- Paper
- Microfiche
- Videos
- Magnetic media

The information can be processed:

- Manually
- Through electronic equipment

When the information is in a magnetic medium and can be processed through a computer, it is called applications.

Parameters for the selection of vital applications

For the purposes of selecting the applications, seven parameters must be taken into account for each of them.

1. Maximum time that can be worked without that application.

2. Information dependency.

3. Relationship with other processes.

4. Unit with facilities and equipment.

5. Staff experience.

6. Financial impact.

7. Security requirements.

Vital Applications Selection Questionnaire

Name of the application. Use a form for each application	
Owner:	
1. Maximum time	1. more than two weeks 2. one to two weeks 3. three to seven days Four. up to two days 5. less than eight hours
2. Dependence on information.	1. No further information or support is required 2. Required but can be retrieved from other sources.

	(manual of other applications) 3. Required and cannot be retrieved from another source (requires backup) Four. Required for this and one other application. (requires backup)
3. Dependence on other processes	1. All the information it generates is independent. (For your own use). 2. Generate information for another process. 3. It generates its own information and for another process. Four. Generate information for a vital process 5. It generates its own information and for a vital process.
4. Dependency on facilities and equipment (SW and HW)	1. The application does not require them. 2. Requires them but they can be obtained elsewhere 3. It requires the facilities. Four. Requires equipment 5. It requires facilities and equipment.
5. Experience of the staff maintaining the application	1. It doesn't matter the level of experience. 2. Staff must have a minimum of experience. 3. The experience required is minimal and training is required. Four. It must be staff with a good level of experience.

	5. Staff must be trained and experienced.
6. Financial impact	1. Null 2. Is minimal 3. It is contemplated in the risks Four. It is tolerable but impacts image with third parties 5. It is very large and cannot be tolerated
7. Information security	1. belongs to the public domain 2. any employee can have access to it 3. its disclosure may affect financially Four. may affect third parties 5. only certain employees should access it

Vital Records Program

Generalities

Purpose

Establish a program to identify those records that contain vital information of the company, in order to protect them according to an efficient procedure and guarantee their availability in test and emergency situations. Additionally, its objectives are:

1. Safeguard the interests of the company.
2. Protect evidence of shareholder ownerships.
3. Maintain the rights and interests of employees.
4. Ensure the fulfillment of commitments with clients

Program Owner

Usually falls to the records and information manager but can be taken over by another function, for example the archive

Application

To all groups, operating units and corporate support. The legal requirements specified in contracts or with the government must be respected.

The information is or is not vital, there is no middle ground. If the company can go back to business without this information, even with difficulties, the information should not be viewed as vital.

Do not confuse vital information with useful information, it is impractical. Costly and unnecessary to try to protect all the information that we would like to have for the restoration of the operation.

Do not choose information because of its historical value or because of government retention laws.

The procedure for analyzing each record to determine whether it should be classified as vital may have several shortcomings. For example.

1. There is a tendency to select records that are not currently vital. (they probably were)

2. Some records that are needed in disaster recovery are missing, as they are not required during operation.

3. There are records that may not be inventoried because they exist inside the desks or on a separate microcomputer.

4. There is a temptation to select entire files only to duplicate them, when only a few are vital.

Identification methods.

There are several methods of identifying records that contain vital information. The functional method will be used as it is the most complete and provides a simpler program.

Guide to Selecting Vital Records

When selecting a record that contains vital information, there are many questions that can serve as a guide.

- What functions are going to be rebuilt after a contingency?
- What corporate assets and evidence of shareholder ownership will they protect?
- Can extra copies be created? Are these copies distributed in the normal course of business? It is this satisfactory distribution.
- Are there other records that contain the same information?
- How quickly is information needed after the disaster?
- Where will the information be needed?

A disaster can be caused by fire, flood, earthquake and other emergency situation, such as civil unrest, demonstration, military action and other man-made threats. For example, someone may press the wrong button and erase a tape or mistakenly send a file to a location other than where it should be, or get lost during transport etc. Some of these errors can be voluntary or involuntary.

Protection of Records

The protection method selected will depend on how the registry is constructed, how it will be used, the need for it after an emergency, and the degree of protection required.

Local storage protection. Local protection of records is acceptable as long as they are stored in a separate building that meets the protection conditions. Storage in the locality. Normally keeping the logs on a day-to-day basis is not preferred because the logs are not immediately accessible after a disaster and it may take a long time before accessing this site.

Distributed storage protection. Provide protection of the records by sending their copies to other locations that will not be affected by the disaster. Eg. In another branch.

Prefabricated Distribution. Through the day-to-day operation of the company, the records and their copies are prepared and distributed to other areas and locations for their use and reference.

Improvised Distribution. When the records are duplicated at the time of creation, with the express purpose of being stored for security reasons in another location.

Protection by reduction or copying. When certain records are impractical to be copied, due to their volume or because multiple copies are required, one must resort to copying or duplicating on microfiche, or reducing photocopies.

Protection for maintenance of the original. By sending the originals of the records to vital records storage when the original is no longer needed for the normal purposes of the operation, you avoid multiplicity of copies when the records are too voluminous.

Vital Records Warehouse Features

1. Security against illegal access and disclosure to unauthorized persons.

2. Safety against steam, fire, flood, excessive heat, and other destructive agents.

3. Ease of access to records

4. Protection in the locality.

Programming

Records must be protected according to an authorized plan. Continuous and consistent of an approved vital records schedule. This will serve as a guide to show which records will go to the warehouse and when they will be updated.

List all records selected as vital in the vital records schedule. Describe the entire contents of the record. I did not submit the schedule until I received approval from the department and records management. Distribute copies of the vital records schedule to people who need it to take action.

- Copy. No. 1 - To the person responsible for the vital records program in the locality of origin.

- Copy No. 2 - to the records manager of the division or country

- Copy No. 3 - To the operational department responsible for the registry

- Copy No. 4 - To the security store in a sealed envelope.

- Copy No. 5 - to the central record store (if any)

Vital record storage

1. Shipment of records to warehouse

2. Packaging of the records for shipment to the secure

warehouse

3. Distribution of the control form and its copies.

4. An index of the records in the warehouse is required for easy retrieval in case of contingency. One suggested form of archiving may be vital records scheduling.

Update and destruction of vital records

The vital information protected in the warehouse must be constantly updated. The restoration of operations as well as the protection of assets, depends on having the information in its most recent update

Vital records must be kept in the warehouse until they are replaced by more up-to-date ones, or until it is determined that they have lost vital characteristics, either due to changes in the operation or because they were poorly defined.

Preparation of the Vital Records schedule

Clearly identify the records to include in this schedule. Include specific instructions for each block of information as shown below.

1. Division. Department, section, office.

2. Location. The location for which the schedule is prepared, for example the plant, office, laboratory. Etc.

3. Registration number. Generate a number for each

record within the same location.

4.   Record Title and Description: The record name including the form number, if available. The shape number alone is not enough. Prepare a short description if the title of the record is not clear enough for a person unfamiliar with the record and its operation.

5.   Please indicate the form of protection.

6.   Indicate the storage location. Where records are stored for protection purposes.

7.   Upgrade. Indicate how often a new copy of the vital record is sent to the warehouse. Weekly, monthly etc.

8.   Retention. Indicate how long the record should be kept in the warehouse. Use the following encoding.

Permanent: records will be designated for permanent retention only if the information is classified as vital for the life of the company.

Termination: The record will be removed from the warehouse after its termination or a specific number of years after it.

Years: The specific number of years of your retention.

By update: many security records are vital only until they are replaced by updated data.

Program review criteria

When reviewing the vital records program, the following questions are worth asking.

1. When the last audit of the program was carried out locally and outside of it.

2. Examine the procedure by which all records are periodically identified as vital or not by their owners. Is the frequency of copying sufficient to meet the owner's requirement for the shortest time to recover?

3. The need for backup copies is specified during the system design process. Check this on a system that is currently under development.

4. Access to the backup storage location is controlled and limited to authorized individuals only. How can you verify them?

5. Test the care effectiveness of a backing tape requirement. Do it randomly.

6. Inspect the document that indicates when the records were sent to the backup storage location. When was the last shipment? They are periodic shipments, who is the person responsible for the integrity of the shipments? Who is responsible when this person is on vacation?

7. Examine the listings for what is supposed to be out of town. Pick a manageable percentage at random. Go to

the backup storage location and determine if all the chosen records can be located. Determine if any of these contain the correct information, with the correct dates and without access errors.

8. A good test of the integrity and real purpose of the vital registration program is to run a testing process locally. All the information to be entered must be obtained from the warehouse.

9. How quickly can the facility be ready to test any vital processes after they are required?

10.

Work teams

Features for integration

Each team has specific goals along with a plan to accomplish. The sum of the individual teams' plans constitutes the business recovery plan. The managing team specifies the working relationships for all teams. Teams usually do not work under "disaster" circumstances. Although disaster recovery teams should be activated immediately when a disaster has been declared.

Team activities

Each team has a specific mission as soon as the disaster is declared: this mission takes precedence over any other job until the disaster has been declared "finished". The reporting structure between work teams should be established in advance.

Each team leader and all other members working in the data process or in the user area become full-time members of the team, that is, their only responsibility will be those of the team. The management team may or may not include the leaders of the other teams, depending on the need.

Responsibilities of team leaders

- Prepare and review the work, at least twice a year, or when a major change related to the team occurs and when required by the management team.

- Read the disaster recovery plan documentation with particular attention to the areas pertaining to your equipment.

- Ensure that the necessary material of the disaster equipment is reliable, current and meets the standards of the plan.

- Ensure that "gray areas" of responsibility cease to exist.

- Whenever appropriate, fulfill specific responsibilities designated for your team.

Selection of team members

It is recommended to start with the list of teams, their description and responsibilities. Try to follow the current structure of the organization so that the responsibilities are familiar.

Build on the people you have, not who you could count on or train on. Interview your staff, classify them by Systems and programs familiar to them, as well as their level of training.

Include users and administrative personnel who normally handle data processing and Information Systems. This inventory should be useful during process analysis and internal process design of system operation.

Cross-train your staff in different jobs and locations as much as possible to ensure the availability of specialized and critical skills.

The work teams. Its mission and functions

Administrator Team

Its mission is to ensure that normal services are restored within the expected times. Your pre-disaster planning responsibilities are:

a. Make decisions about total strategy and recovery, after reconciling the point of view of the user and senior management.

b. Review project reports, proposals and plans for other teams as they are produced.

c. Make sure the recovery plan is kept up to date.

The functions during the disaster are:

a. Declare that the recovery plan will be implemented.

b. Depending on the information provided by the rescue team, it decides the use of the alternate center, thus communicating with the service provider and specifying the requirements.

c. Instruct the warehouse team leader to get all vital paper documents available from the off-site warehouse.

d. List the availability of all company employees.

e. Decide on team leaders and alternate members if necessary.

f. Put a copy of all the material in the command post.

g. Tell your equipment, program, and application leaders when to start with your installation plan.

h. Decide on the location of the command post.

i. Manage the recovery plan from the command post.

j. Give guidance to the leaders of other teams.

k. Keep the director or senior management (person in charge of external statements) informed.

The administrative services team

Its mission is to ensure that all administrative and communication services are available to teams during the recovery period. Also, you must ensure that lists of administrative service users' requirements are available immediately after the disaster.

The responsibilities before the disaster are:

a. Test the ability to carry out the functions assigned to it during the disaster.

b. Coordinate your task with the other teams and review it with the management team.

The functions during the disaster are:

a. Adapt the command post with the appropriate ones.

b. Provide transportation to people, equipment,

facilities.

c. Provide office services with updated lists of requirements.

d. Communicate phone numbers and command post location to all team members and department heads in all divisions of the company.

e. Provide alternative means for person-to-person communication, such as cell phones or radio, in the event that normal telephone service is not available.

f. Provide the welfare of the recovery staff, for example, lodging, food, personal transportation, maps, diagrams of the locations where the recovery will take place.

g. Ensure staff overtime is recorded.

h. Hire temporary staff if required.

i. Arrangement for expenses, payment of bills and payroll.

j. Arrangement for photocopying.

k. Keep the Administrator team informed of your activity.

The Applications Team

Its mission is to ensure that any critical application is processed within the established time. Also, ensure that each application is restored without loss of vital records. Finally, restore the applications as specified.

Responsibilities before disaster:

- Ensure plans for backup and restoration of any vital application are complete, reflect changes as they occur, and are validated for reliability twice a year through off-site testing.

- Work with the warehouse team to ensure that the various forms of backup are safe and organized for quick retrieval.

- Work with operations teams and programs to ensure that changes from working in a different location do not impact.

- Write a plan for the backup of each vital application. Also, write the test script and test the plan.

- Write a plan for the restoration of each vital application. That is, a separate procedure for each application.

Duties during the disaster:

- For all applications. Retrieve the necessary documentation and that is planned. Collect and search input forms and documents still in the hands of user departments to determine the selection and limit for re-entering the data.

- For supporting critical applications. Retrieve all the supporting material including the documentation listed in the application backup procedures. Execute the backup procedures for the application with the support of the software team if necessary. Restore to the restored system when necessary.

- For the Restoration of all applications. When the restored system is available, start the "run" of applications in the sequence previously.

The communications team

Its mission is to ensure that communications equipment and lines are available.

The responsibilities before the disaster are:

- Plan and test the ability to establish remote communication from the alternate center.

- Anticipate the need for data telephone lines in the area where remote terminals are installed.

- Maintain alternating network information with characteristics and details for each line.

The functions during the disaster are:

- Verify the operation of the alternate network once the system is restored.

- Sort lines, terminals and modems if required.

- Achieve restoration of data transmission channels.

- Assist the operations team with any change in procedures.

- Test the data transmission channels, verifying the operability with the central computer.

- Assist the operations team to monitor and control the network.

- Keep the administrative team aware of its activity.

The equipment of civil facilities or physical facilities

Its mission is to ensure that the computer center restoration site and other proprietary sites are ready for people and equipment when needed.

Your Responsibilities before the disaster are:

- Plan the adaptation of an alternate restoration location. Cold Site.

- Plan the adaptation of a work area with remote terminals.

Duties during the disaster:

- Work with administrative teamss, communications, hardware and operations as well as with the contractors in the choice and design of the restoration site.

- Prepare floor plans and workflows for the restoration

town.

- Prepare restoration facilities to receive equipment, electricity, telephones, etc.

- Establish security procedures in the restaurant area.

- Coordinate with the salvage team in moving recovered equipment to the restoration location.

- Supervisor of the physical installation of equipment, lines, telephones, furniture, etc.

- Arrange any necessary assistance in the restaurant area to other teams, especially communications.

- Keep the administrative team informed of your activity.

Hardware equipment

Its mission is to have the data processing equipment available when needed. Responsibilities before disaster are:

- Maintain a list of the equipment installed in the company with its characteristics and serial numbers. This information can be shared with the team in chargeof the claim to the insurance company.

The functions during the disaster are:

- Advise the rescue team in the rescue of equipment and validate which is usable and which is not.

- Order the replacements taking into account the above

information.

- Coordinate with software, application, and facility teams on unplanned changes needed to accommodate different hardware.

- Rushing deliveries.

- Cancel orders for equipment replacement immediately if the original is operational.

- Keep the administrative team informed of your activity.

The operations team

Its mission is to ensure that normal processing can take place as soon as the required system, equipment and communications are available.

The responsibilities before the disaster are:

- Ensure that for any data processing supply that cannot be obtained in less than 24 hours, a month's supply is kept in the warehouse outside of the locality.

- Ensure that the custody information is backed up in the warehouse outside the locality, within the specified times.

- Work with operations, program, and communications teams to test application restoration procedures under simulated disaster conditions.

The functions during the disaster are:

- Work with the communications equipment, hardware and facilities in the implementation of the assigned recovery area.

- Have the lists, tapes, discs for which the team is responsible, recovered from the warehouse within the established times.

- Make copies immediately and have the originals out of town without delay.

- Coordinate the work to be done with the communications equipment, hardware and programs while they test.

- Run recovery jobs.

- Keep the administrative team informed of your activity.

Computer equipment or personal systems

Its mission is to have personal computers available when needed.

The responsibilities before the disaster are:

- Maintain a list of the equipment installed in the company with its characteristics and serial numbers. This information may be shared with the insurance claim team.

- Keep copies of PC operating systems.

The functions during the disaster are:

- Advise the rescue team in the rescue of equipment and validate which are usable and which not.

- Order the replacements taking into account the above information.

- Coordinate with software, application, and facility teams on unplanned changes needed to accommodate different hardware.

- Rushing deliveries.

- Cancel orders for equipment replacement immediately if the original is operational.

- Keep the administrative team informed of your activity.

The rescue team

Its mission is to calculate the extent of damage to the company's facilities and equipment. In addition, provide information to the management team for the declaration of the disaster and the selection of alternatives, if any, for the restoration of the process. Finally, recover what can be saved. Pre-disaster responsibilities are those responsibilities specified above.

The functions during the disaster are:

- Establish security in the disaster location.

- Identify the equipment and material to be saved.

- Keep hardware and communications teams informed.

- Prevent consequential damages.

- Provide logistical support to move the salvaged equipment to the new process site.

- Start the claim to the insurance companies

- Keep the administrative team informed of your activity.

The software or Operational Systems team

Its mission is to ensure the operation of the system programs necessary for the restoration site. The responsibilities before the disaster are.

- Plan, prepare and test, as practical, the system programs that may be needed to be used at the restoration site.

- Coordinate with communications, hardware, operations, and applications teams on programs that are hardware-dependent.

- Establish the requirements of the file operating system, libraries and system utilities.

- Ensure that previous changes to system programs are complete, reflect changes when they occur and are valid in their accuracy at the appropriate times in the year.

- Write and test a plan to restore normal process on a fresh hardware system from the factory.

- Take the System offline.

- Simulate a new system by erasing all memories.

- Run the entire plan using only the material recovered from the warehouse outside the locality.

- Restore the system.

- Bring the system online.

- Correct errors and omissions found in out-of-town warehouse vital records scheduling and plan testing.

- Post the test plans and their results in the documentation.

The functions during the disaster are:

- Help the applications team to establish their mini operating systems.

- Ensure that all programs can run on the replacement computer.

- Sort any necessary items from the lists for which the team is responsible.

- Load and test the operating system and other systems and files.

- Coordinate with hardware and communications

teams.

- Keep the administrative team informed of your activity.

Vital Records Storage Equipment

Its mission is to ensure that all retrieval information stored away from the data center is safe and can be easily retrieved by, and only by, authorized persons. The responsibilities before the disaster are:

- Plan, maintain, and regularly test and audit the system that moves vital records to the out-of-site warehouse.

- Work closely with operations teams and Of applications.

The functions during the disaster are:

- Closely monitor the recovery of data backed up to off-site storage locations.

- Make enough copies of this disaster recovery plan for all team leaders, plus one extra copy.

- Deliver all recovered material to the leader of the management team

- Keep the administrative team informed of your activity.

Choice of alternate center

Reciprocal agreement

It is an agreement between the organization and another company, where each company agrees to share the resources of its data center in the event of a disaster.

Advantage

- Low cost.

- Immediate availability of equipment if the other company has excess capacity.

- Effective for requirements in a short period of time.

- Established location with already established expenses (transportation. Food, etc.)

Disadvantages.

- They can be affected by the same disaster.

- Additional equipment and computing time required to accommodate the "partner."

- The hardware and software of each company may not be compatible or have duplication problems.

- Difficulty in obtaining test time.

- It is NOT a long term solution.

- Difficulty obtaining a contractual commitment from the partner.

Reconstruction in an alternate location

A disaster is assumed to have totally destroyed some of the data center sites. The contingency plan addresses the reconstruction of the existing facility or the construction of the new premises.

Advantage

- Long term availability.

- Single owner.

Disadvantages

- Reconstruction and configuration expenses.

- Time lost in rebuilding.

- Installation of equipment needed during this phase.

- Difficulty testing this option except when simulating the disaster.

Corporate agreement

It is an agreement between several members of a corporation that establishes to share available data processing resources with the company that suffers some type of disaster.

Advantage

- Shared costs.

- Cash for problems that are solved in the short term.

- Availability on the basis of the contract.

Disadvantages

- Members can suffer the effects of the same disaster.

- It can be difficult to maintain hardware and software compatibility for all centers. calculation.

- Difficulty in obtaining resources and time for tests.

- Members may be geographically distant, which may increase transportation costs.

Own alternate computer center

Advantage

- Stay for a long period of time.

- Single owner.

- Immediate availability.

- Ease of testing.

Disadvantages

- Expensive.

- Additional investment in equipment calculation.

- Return on investment in the medium term.

Commercial recovery center. Hot Site

It consists of an external company with almost immediate availability of data processing, so that in a temporary period (one or two months) it can be occupied by a company to carry out its recovery plan, while building its own premises.

Advantage

- Immediate availability.

- Medium-term permanence.

- Shared costs.

- Trial time available as part of the service contract.

Disadvantages

- Availability to the limit of clients that can support.

- High costs for overage airtime charges.

- Additional charges for online backup.

- Hardware and software compatibility must be maintained through ongoing reviews.

- Transportation, food and lodging expenses.

Recovery plan test

Generalities

The recovery plan test is the assurance that the business recovery is successful. The tests of the plan are part of its maintenance. This maintenance by testing should include:

1. Recovery test planning.

2. Carrying out the test.

3. Review of the test.

4. Document the problems encountered.

5. Define the action plan to solve the problems.

6. Update the documentation.

When planning the test you should:

1. Determine the level of proof.

   a. Participants

   b. To choose of the test site.

   c. Type of backup to use.

2. Determine the objective of the test.

a. Set the scope of the test. Operating system, Databases, Vital process applications, telecommunications, Total production.

b. Set the revision level. Structured (until achieving the logo), system operability (Test the IPL), By parallels (Compare previous data against updated), Production.

c. Set measurement criteria. By time, by results.

The test modeler

The activities of the modeler before the test are:

1. Review the objectives.

2. Review the proposed scope.

3. Determine the revision level.

4. Choose your support staff.

5. Establish criteria for failing the test.

6. Inform the alternate center when the test will take place.

The activities of the modeler after the test.

1. Ask for feedback from the staff who participated.

2. Give recommendations to improve / update the plan.

3. It ensures that unnecessary information is destroyed.

4. Makes recommendations on detected problem areas.

5. Generate a document with the test results.

6. Help support for plan modifications.

.

Bibliography

Fallara, P. Disaster Recovery Planning. IEEE Potentials. 2004, Vol. 22, No. 5, pp. 42-44.

Hayes, PE and. Hammons, A. Disaster Recovery Project Management. Proceedings of IEEE 47th Petroleum and Chemical Industry Conference, Sep. 2000, pp. 55-63.

ICONTEC (2009). GTC 176. Guide for business continuity management (BCM)

ICONTEC (2009). Compendium, Information Security Management System (ISMS) - Second Edition

McCarthy, NK Todd, Matthew. Klaben, Jeff (2012). The Computer Incident Response Planning Handbook: Executable Plans for Protecting Information at Risk 1st Edition, Kindle Edition. McGraw-Hill Education; 1 edition. 240 pages

Rothstein, Philip Jan. Disaster Recovery Testing: Exercising Your Contingency Plan (2007 Edition) 2007th Edition. Rothstein Associates Inc.

Rudolph, CG Business Continuation Planning / Disaster Recovery: a Marketing Perspective, IEEE Communications Magazine, 1990, Vol. 28, No. 6, pp. 25-28.

Wallace, Michael. Webber, Lawrence. (2017). The Disaster Recovery Handbook: A Step-by-Step Plan to Ensure Business Continuity and Protect Vital Operations, Facilities, and Assets Kindle Edition. AMACOM; 3 edition

Wilson Bautista Jr. (2018). Practical Cyber Intelligence: How action-based intelligence can be an effective response to incidents. Packt Publishing. 316 p

www.ingramcontent.com/pod-product-compliance
Lightning Source LLC
Chambersburg PA
CBHW051114050326
40690CB00006B/788